Young people discover the cycle of plant growth through this rhythmic story dance.

Tick, Tock, the Popcorn Clock

By Jane Belk Moncure

Illustrated by
Helen Endres

THE
CHILD'S
WORLD
ELGIN, ILLINOIS 60120

26720

Library of Congress Cataloging in Publication Data

Moncure, Jane Belk.
    Tick, tock, the popcorn clock.

    (Creative dramatics)
    SUMMARY: Children enact the cycle of popcorn growing
from its seeds into tall stalks, under the care of the
farmer, and finally being picked and thrown into the
popcorn pot for eating.
    [1. Popcorn—Fiction] I. Endres, Helen. II. Title.
III. Series.
PZ7.M739Ti   [E]   77-13120
ISBN 0-89565-010-X

Distributed by Childrens Press, 1224 West Van Buren Street, Chicago,
Illinois 60607.

Tick, Tock, the Popcorn Clock

The farmer plants some popcorn seeds.

He rakes the ground.

He pulls the weeds.

7

While deep in the ground, the popcorn seeds
sleep,
sleep,
sleep.

Tick, tock, time goes by.
Puffy clouds fill up the sky
and sprinkle the earth with rain.

Then sunshine dries the earth again
and warms the little seeds.

They wake up very slowly. . .
oh, so very slowly. . .
stretching their finger-like stems,
reaching into the sunshine,

11

pushing their toe-like roots
way down into the ground.

Now they are anchored in the ground.
Two by two, new leaves appear.

The corn stalks swing
                            and sway
                                        and rock,
tick, tock, like popcorn clocks,
on a bright, warm, summer day.

Summer ticks away.
Each corn stalk wears a tassel crown,

nods and waves,
    nods and waves,

and bends the tassels up and down
as if to say, "Please come and play."

The blackbirds come, but not to play!
They come to eat!

And they stay until
the farmer chases them away.

Tick, tock, time goes by.
Thunder rumbles in the sky.

Corn stalks twist in the wind,
then turn around and twist again
and tumble almost to the ground.

At last the angry storm blows past.
Corn stalks lift branches full of corn
and dance and dance in the sunshine warm.

Now it is fall. Wild geese call.
The corn stands tall, tiptoe tall.

The corn is ripe
and ready to eat.
The farmer picks popcorn
for a treat.

"Everyone join hands," says he.
"Let's have a big, round husking bee!"

Tick, tock, sounds the popcorn clock.
Hop around the popcorn clock;
circle around the popcorn clock.

Right in the middle is the popcorn pot!
Trot around the popcorn pot.

Throw in the popcorn. Watch it pop!
Pop!
Pop!
Pop!

Tiptoe around the popcorn pot.
Smell the popcorn, sizzling hot.

Squat down around the popcorn pot
and eat the popcorn while it's hot.

About the Author:

Jane Belk Moncure, author of many books and stories for young children, is a graduate of Virginia Commonwealth University and Columbia University. She has taught nursery, kindergarten and primary children in Europe and America. Mrs. Moncure has taught early childhood education while serving on the faculties of Virginia Commonwealth University and the University of Richmond. She was the first president of the Virginia Association for Early Childhood Education and has been recognized widely for her services to young children. She is married to Dr. James A. Moncure, Vice President of Elon College, and currently lives in Burlington, North Carolina.

About the Artist:

Helen Endres is a commercial artist, designer and illustrator of children's books. She has lived and worked in the Chicago area since coming from her native Oklahoma in 1952. Graduated from Tulsa University with a BA, she received further training at Hallmark in Kansas City and from the Chicago Art Institute. Ms. Endres attributes much of her creative achievement to the advice and encouragement of her Chicago contemporaries and to the good humor and patience of the hundreds of young models who have posed for her.

Creative dramatics provides a framework for the expression of many emotions and thoughts. Children are constantly dramatizing events that have happened to them, characters and situations they have seen on television, and happenings people have discussed with them. Through imaginative play, a child restructures his own experiences and discovers new ones. By imitating others in play, he comes to understand what they do and why, and also how their actions affect him.